200

Religious Topics

RELIGIOUS DRESS

Jon Mayled

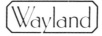

Religious Topics

Birth Customs
Death Customs
Family Life
Feasting and Fasting
Festivals
Holy Books
Initiation Rites
Marriage Customs

Pilgrimage
Religious Art
Religious Dress
Religious Food
Religious Services
Religious Symbols
Religious Teachers and Prophets

Editor: Deborah Elliott

Cover: Young *Mahayana*
Buddhist monks wearing the
traditional red robes.

First published in 1987 by Wayland (Publishers) Limited
61 Western Road, Hove, East Sussex, England BN3 1JD

© Copyright 1987 Wayland (Publishers) Limited

British Library Cataloguing in Publication Data
Mayled, Jon
  Religious dress. – (Religious topics)
  1. Religious costume – Juvenile literature
  I. Title   II. Series
  291.3   BL603
  ISBN 0–85078–775–0

In this book, wherever we have
used dates we have used the
abbreviations CE and BCE. These
refer to the Common Era: after the
year 1 when Jesus was born; and
Before the Common Era.

Phototypeset by Kalligraphics Ltd., Redhill, Surrey
Printed in Italy by G. Canale & C.S.p.A., Turin
Bound in the UK at the Bath Press, Avon

Contents

Introduction

If you are going out to a party or some other special occasion you will probably want to dress up in special clothes. These clothes make the occasion seem more important and make you feel very special about going to it.

The five Sikh men in this procession are members of the Khalsa, *the unity of the Sikh brotherhood. They are wearing the traditional saffron robes, turbans and are carrying* kirpans *(swords).*

Young Catholic girls traditionally wear white for their first Holy Communion. This is the Christian religious ceremony which commemorates the last supper which Jesus ate with his disciples.

In the same way many people who follow the world's religions wear special clothes when they are about to worship their God or gods, or perhaps they will wear clothes every day which show that they belong to a special religion or religious group.

In this book we shall look at the clothes which ordinary people wear for their religion and also those which the leaders of their religious groups wear. You will see that in all the major religions of the world there are rules and traditions about the clothes which are worn.

Buddhism

Buddhist worshippers do not wear any special dress but the monks or *bhikkus*, do.

A young man who wishes to become a monk is called a *naag*. On the day before he is admitted to the monastery, he travels through the streets under a large umbrella wearing a white robe to show that his wish to become a monk is pure. Before the ceremony all the hair, including his eyebrows, is shaved off the young man's face. He leaves home wearing a cone-shaped hat and a net robe richly decorated with gold. This symbolizes the life of the *Buddha* when he was living as a prince in Lumbini.

When the *naag* arrives at the *wat* (monastery) he removes these rich clothes. The other monks then give him the monk's robes which he will wear. He is also given a blanket, begging bowl, razor and a pair of sandals.

A young Buddhist preparing for life in the monastery.

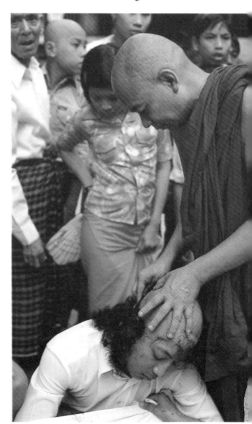

6

A naag travelling to the monastery. He is dressed in rich clothes to symbolize the life of the Buddha when he was a Prince.

There are two schools of Buddhism, *Theravada* and *Mahayana*. Buddhists of the *Theravada* school wear orange robes and *Mahayana* Buddhists wear red robes.

Young Nepali children dressed in ceremonial Buddhist costume.

Young Buddhist monks in the traditional orange robes of the Theravada *school of* Buddhism.

Christianity

In most Christian churches the minister or priest will wear special clothes. In a Protestant church or chapel these may be just a long black gown over a dark suit. The minister may also wear a white band around his neck called a clerical collar or 'dog collar' with two pieces of white cloth hanging down from it. These are known as preaching tabs.

In Roman Catholic and some Anglican churches the priests wear very special clothes for services. As well as their clerical collars, they have full-length, tight-fitting black coats called cassocks or soutanes.

For ordinary services priests cover their cassocks with a large white garment, known as a surplice if it is long and a cotta if it is short. Over this they have a long band of coloured cloth called a stole. On very special days they may also wear a cope, which is a

This Roman Catholic priest in Kenya is wearing the traditional red and black robes of a cardinal (one of the advisors to the Pope).

long cape usually made of beautifully embroidered cloth.

When they are celebrating the Eucharist priests cover their cassocks with a tight-fitting white robe known as an alb. This is tied around the waist with a rope called the girdle. Around their necks they have a square of cloth called an amice. This is worn under the alb. Over this is the stole and then a chasuble, which is embroidered like a cope but goes over the neck and is open on both sides.

This Anglican minister (centre) is pictured with members of his choir and congregation. He is wearing a cassock with a cotta over the top.

These clothes are worn to show how special the Eucharist is. The colour of the stole, chasuble and cope varies according to the season of the church's year and any particular festival which is being celebrated.

When a bishop visits a church he wears a cope. On his head is a tall stiff hat called a mitre and he may wear special gloves. He carries a long silver or gold shepherd's crook.

The Bishop of Evreux wearing a mitre and a chasuble.

Left *A church procession in Cologne, West Germany. It is interesting to note the variety of clothes worn by the Roman Catholic clergy.*

Christian monks and nuns also wear special clothes, though nowadays some may wear ordinary clothes. Their traditional long robes are called habits. The cords around their waists have three knots representing the vows of poverty, chastity and obedience which they have made. Some monks have their heads shaved in the centre. This is called a tonsure. Nuns keep their heads covered with a veil and wimple.

These nuns at a mission in Kenya are wearing grey and white habits.

Hinduism

Hindus do not wear any special clothes for worship but some may wear long, loose garments called *dhotis*.

The three highest castes for Hindu men are the Brahmins, Kshatriyas and Vaisyas. They

The men at this Hindu religious procession are wearing dhotis, *long loose garments.*

are called twice-born because they are 'born again' in the *Upanayana* or Sacred Thread ceremony. This takes place when a boy is between the ages of eight and sixteen. A sacred thread is placed on his left shoulder by a Guru

These Hindu women are wearing brightly coloured saris. Saris are traditional dress for Indian women.

or teacher. The thread hangs across his chest down to his right thigh. The thread contains fine single strands. These are white, red and yellow and are tied with a spiritual knot called the *Brahma Granthi*. The three strands are said to represent the gods Brahma, Vishnu and Shiva.

When Hindus are praying they may mark their foreheads with a *tilak* mark. This is made from a red paste. The *tilak* will show which god a person worships. For example, three horizontal lines are the symbol of Shiva and three vertical lines the symbol of Vishnu.

Above *A Hindu priest. The vertical marks on his forehead show that he is a follower of Vishnu.*

Worshippers at a religious ceremony in Malacca.

These Hindu worshippers are at a temple ceremony in Bali. It is interesting to see all the richly coloured clothes worn by the worshippers.

Islam

The rules about Muslim dress come from the *Qur'an* (the Muslim holy book) and apply to everyday life as well as prayer. Most Muslims wear clothes which are traditional either in the country that their families come from or where they are now living.

Men must keep themselves covered from the navel to the knees. They can choose whether or not they wish to wear head coverings for prayer. Unlike women, men are not allowed to wear clothes containing pure silver or gold. Men and women must not wear clothes designed for each other. Shoes are not worn in the mosque. In some countries women must cover the whole of their bodies apart from their faces and hands and their clothes should be loose-fitting. Once girls are teenagers many of them keep their faces covered when going out or meeting strangers.

Muslim boys wearing prayer hats of a traditional design.

Muslim worshippers must not wear shoes in a mosque.

This is called *purdah*.

When Muslims make the *Hajj*, (pilgrimage to Mecca) they all wear two white sheets of

This Muslim woman from Oman has her head and face covered because she is in purdah. Purdah *is the custom in some Muslim communities, of women wearing clothing that conceals them completely when they go out.*

seamless cloth called *ihram*. This shows that they are all equal before God.

At the festival of *Id al-Fitr*, which marks the end of the month long fast of *Ramadan*, it is usual for Muslims to wear new clothes to celebrate.

These pilgrims at Mecca are wearing ihram, *two white sheets of seamless cotton, for the* Hajj.

Judaism

Religious dress is a very important part of Judaism and the basis for this can be found in the *Tenakh*, the Jewish holy scriptures.

Orthodox (strict) Jewish men keep their heads covered at all times by a small cap.

At a Jewish wedding the bride wears white and the groom wears a dark suit and a kittel.

This cap is called a *kippah* or *yarmulkah*. Very strict Orthodox women also keep their heads covered with a *sheitel*, which can be a scarf or in somes cases a wig. Most Jewish women cover their heads at home when lighting the candles for the *Sabbath*.

At prayer, Jewish men wear a *tallit* or prayer shawl. These white shawls have black or blue stripes at the ends and tassels and fringes. The 613 strands and knots which make up the tassels represent the number of laws in the *Torah*. For prayer men wear two small black leather boxes with thongs attached called *tefillin* or phylacteries. The *tefillin shel rosh* is worn on the forehead and the *tefillin shel yad* on the left arm. In the boxes are small scrolls of parchment containing passages from the *Torah*. Some Orthodox Jewish men wear a garment called a *tzitzit*. This is a rectangular piece of white cloth with strings at the four corners which is placed over the head.

A family of traditionally dressed Hassidic Jews at the Western Wall in Jerusalem.

A young boy learning to put on tefillin *in preparation for his Bar Mitzvah (initiation ceremony).*

During the festival of *Yom Kippur* Jews do not wear leather shoes and many men also wear a long, loose white gown, called a *kittel*, in the synagogue. This may represent a shroud and shows that they are humbling themselves before God.

The community of Hassidic Jews is very strict. Hassidic Jews observe the Biblical law in Leviticus of not cutting off the corners of their hair. Because of this they allow the hair over their ears to grow down in long curls. Hassidic women always keep their heads covered and only wear dresses with sleeves which come down to their elbows.

An Hassidic boy in Jerusalem with curls of hair over his ears. According to the Book of Leviticus, Jews may not cut off the corners of their hair.

25

Sikhism

Sikhs observe five symbols of their religion which are known as the Five K's.

Kesh – This means that Sikhs do not cut their hair or beards. The uncut hair is a symbol of devotion to God and of living according to his will. Sikhs must wash their hair every four days.

Sikhs who observe the Five K's, the symbols of their religion, do not cut their hair or beards. This is known as kesh. *These Sikh men are wearing turbans to cover their hair.*

Men keep their hair covered by a turban and when Sikhs attend services at the *gurdwara*, or temple, both men and women have their hair covered. Women wear a scarf called a *dupatta*.

This market in Amritsar in India is selling kangas *(combs) and* karas *(steel bracelets).*

This Sikh boy is holding a kirpan, *a small sword worn to show that Sikhs are ready to defend their faith when necessary.*

Kanga – The *kanga* is a comb which is used to keep the hair in place under the turban and is a sign of discipline.

Kachs – These are white shorts which are worn under other clothes. They replaced the long *dhotis* which Hindus wear and show that Sikhs are free of the religious rules of Hinduism.

Kara – Sikhs wear a steel bracelet on their right wrist. It is a symbol of strength and reminds Sikhs of the unity of the *Khalsa*. The *Khalsa* is the brotherhood of Sikhs.

Kirpan – The kirpan is a small sword. This is worn to show that Sikhs are ready to defend their faith when necessary. In many countries it is illegal to carry such a sword and so today many Sikhs have a very small dagger as part of the decoration of the *kanga*.

Apart from the Five K's and the turban and dupatta there is no special religious dress for Sikhs. Although most men wear ordinary European dress many Sikh women wear traditional dress from the Punjab such as *shalwar* (long, baggy trousers) and *khameeze* (a tunic). Shoes are not worn in the *gurdwara*, the Sikh temple.

This Sikh bridegroom has his face covered by a silver and gold veil.

Glossary

Bhikkus Theravada Buddhist monks. They can be recognized by their orange robes and shaved heads.

Brahma Granthi A sacred spiritual knot.

Cassock An ankle-length garment, usually black, worn by priests.

Caste The division of Hindu society into groups which are ranked one above the other.

Chasuble A richly decorated garment worn by priests.

Eucharist A Christian service which remembers the Last Supper Jesus ate with his disciples before he died.

Hassidic Jews A sect of Orthodox (strict) Jews.

Id al-Fitr Festival to mark the end of the fast of Ramadan.

Kesh This is uncut hair, including the beard, which should not be trimmed or shaved, a symbol of the Sikh religion.

Kittel A white garment worn by Jewish men.

Mitre A hat worn by a bishop.

Ramadan The ninth month of the Muslim calendar. A period of dawn to dusk fasting.

Tefillin Small leather boxes containing religious texts, worn on the forehead and left arm.

Tonsure Shaving the top of the head.

Upanayana A Hindu initiation ceremony.

Wimple A piece of cloth draped around the head to frame the face, worn by nuns.

Yom Kippur An annual Jewish High Holy Day.

Further Reading

If you would like to find out more about religious dress you may like to read some of the books in the following series:

Beliefs and Believers series – published by Wayland.

Exploring Religion series – published by Bell and Hyman

Religions of the World series – published by Wayland

Worship series – published by Holt Saunders

The following videos are very helpful:

The Jesus Project – produced by CEM Video.

Through the Eyes series – produced by CEM Video, 2 Chester House, Pages Lane, London, N10.

Acknowledgements

The publisher would like to thank the following for providing pictures for the book: Sally & Richard Greenhill 23, 28; Hutchison library 4, 6, 7, 9, 10, 12 (above), 13, 18, 20, 25, 26, 29; Christine Osborne 21; Anne and Bury Peerless 8, 14, 27; Topham 16 (right), 17; Wayland Picture Library 11; Zefa 5, 12 (left), 15, 16 (above), 19, 22, 24.

Index